The Sun Will Shine Again

The Sun Will Shine Again

Life Lessons from a Year of Grieving

Sissy Taran

Warm wishes,
Sissy Taran

2008 • BERNDOG PUBLISHING, SANTA BARBARA, CALIFORNIA

Published by Berndog Publishing
Post Office Box 5829
Santa Barbara, CA 93150

Book design & Production:
Eric Larson, Studio E Books, Santa Barbara
Set in Bembo

ISBN: 978-0-615-16412-0

08 09 10 11 12   1 2 3 4 5

SUGGESTED SUBJECT CATALOG HEADINGS
Taran, Sissy.
  The sun will shine again : life lessons from a year of grieving / by Sissy
Taran.
    p.   cm.
1. Grief—recovery. 2. Bereavement. 3. Grief—religious aspects.
4. Self-help.   I. Title.

To all my guardian angels,
past and present

ACKNOWLEDGMENTS

The day Bernie and I were at the hospital and learned his diagnosis, it was serendipitous that Rabbi Steve Cohen was there. That put Rabbi Steve with us at the very moment that Bernie began fighting for his life. Again, fortuitously, he was there at Bernie's last breath. No one could have been more perfect as my "interviewer" to help me bring my story out. Without my friend and spiritual guide, without the world's greatest listener, without the beautiful soul of Rabbi Steve, my growth, this journey and this book could never have happened. I will be eternally grateful to him for "walking the walk" with me as we grew, tear by tear, laugh by laugh, together.

I turned to my friend and neighbor, Laurie Deans Medjuck, a writer and editor, because I had no idea how to write a book. When seven months of conversation had been transcribed, she fearlessly waded into the material to shape it (and reshape and reshape it again). She made my vision and dream come alive. There are few people in one's life who will contribute one year of their creativity to help another. Laurie did that. Not only did it, but wanted to do it. No one has appreciated her more. Thank you, too, Joe, for never making me feel guilty about sharing Laurie's time.

There are so many others who have helped with the project along the way:

Mary Lou Kravetz: Thanks for the endless hours of transcribing, and for your much-valued librarian skills, along with your thoughtful comments and encouragement. And a huge hug to Gary for his wisdom, patience, and financial expertise.... Linda Schwartz: You are a master at hand-holding. You moved, shook and helped get the book into print and beyond.... Sarah Songer: Hugs for beginning the transcribing process. I know it wasn't easy.... Heidi Kirkpatrick: Thanks for capturing my treasured memories and objects through photography.... Pam Larsson Toscher: You turned my "kvetching bear" into a masterpiece of pen and ink.... Susan LeVine: You created the beautiful cover painting that captured my vision.... Helene Glassman: For my cover photo you made me look good, and like a real author!... Pam VanBlaricum: I am grateful to my "errorless" CALM (Child Abuse Listening and Mediation) sister who proofread it all.... Carolyn Gillio, Meredith Scott, Marty Silverman: Thanks for helping get the book out to readers.

I also want to thank the following people who recalled stories and memories: Stella Kovacs, an angel who arrived just when I needed her; Constance McClain, my "breathing guru"; Nancy McCoy Carr, the keeper of my childhood memories; cousins Linda Reis and Sharon Triguiero, for sharing family stories.

I must acknowledge those wonderful people in my life who have been there all along: To my knights in shining armor, Michael Schwartz and Ed Martin: You are both special men who have saved me many times.... To my community of friends at Hadassah, CALM, B'nai B'rith Lodge, Congregation B'nai B'rith and ADL: You encompass the true meaning of friendship and love.

To my children, Tiffany, Francine and Nadine: You are my best listeners, critics and appreciators. You have helped me "shine on." And I couldn't ask for better sons-in-law than Scott and Zach: Life is joyous with you.... To my dear grandson, Ethan: You always speak the truth. To Blythe: You represent the cycle of life. May you embody Buddie's and Bernie's spirits.

To my guardian angel father: You proved that an old dog can learn new tricks. Thanks for always loving me and for the indelible memories.... To my guardian angel mother, who told me, "I gave you life, you gave me immortality": Mother, you will never know how much more you gave me.

And to my dearest guardian angel husband: I loved walking hand-in-hand with you. Thank you for all the memories I will forever cherish.

Contents

A section of photographs follows page 92

Foreword

Walking a Shared Path of Learning

WHEN I think back to the moment I decided to become a rabbi, the element most important in that decision was the opportunity to be close to people at profound moments in their lives. Now, as the leader of a 650-family strong congregation, nothing in my work as a rabbi is more important than supporting people in grief. So when Sissy asked me if I would spend time in conversation with her as part of her book project, I saw it as an opportunity to have a very good ongoing conversation with somebody I really respect, and whose thinking I respect, about a crucial piece of my work.

On an intellectual level, I saw it as an educational opportunity. Because I had never lost a close family member in my 50 years—perhaps putting me at a disadvantage in grief counseling—I hoped our conversation would give me deeper insight into this profound dimension of the human experience. On the "heart" level, I anticipated establishing a deeper closeness. The job of rabbi is wonderful because of the opportunity to get close to people, but there is something troubling about the fact that you get close to people and then move on, then get close to other people and move on. Sissy's proposal of seven months of weekly conversations posed a very wonderful opportunity: a chance to stick with the closeness.

During our many months of discussion, Sissy shared with me in a different way than any congregant has ever shared before. As the weeks went by, it became more and more true that our conversations were an important part of my education as a rabbi. Together we walked a path of learning, sharing the wisdom to be gained from the profound and challenging experience of losing a loved one.

From the outset I marveled at how Sissy remained strong when the world was collapsing around her. Our very honest conversations over the months confirmed to me that Sissy seemed to have found a powerful way of moving through a frightening time; that she had put together an approach of how to return to life.

Through Sissy I've witnessed the healing power of a family in a new way, and seen how a family can carry each member through a loss like this. As I watched Sissy choose to trust others and the world at large—rather than close herself off and shut out what had become an untrustworthy world—I saw the healing that comes when a mourner, despite their grief and vulnerability, opens up to friends and community. From our discussions I realized that a rabbi doesn't have to always be the sage and have the perfect thing to say. And, also, that the right thing is to be there in a crisis and trust that people will find a way to let me know when they need privacy.

Most importantly, it became very clear to me that in grief every person is unique, and that there are no rules about what we are supposed to think or feel or say. Even though there are many elements to the mourning process that seem to be common to everybody, it's completely impossible to predict how someone is going to be feeling at any point. Grieving, I've learned, is an individual journey, and there are no shortcuts. Each mourner must make his or her journey, on his or her own terms, in his or her own time.

For all of these lessons, I will always be grateful to my friend Sissy, and to the Compassionate One who every day is healing her broken heart.

—Rabbi Steve Cohen
Congregation B'nai B'rith
Santa Barbara, California

Introduction

Authoring My New Existence

I DID NOT start out on this journey to become an expert on grieving! But when Bernie, my wonderful husband, my friend and partner of nearly three decades, died suddenly from a rare form of stomach cancer, my world was torn apart. Overnight I found myself on a new path, an unexpected journey.

Bernie and I had been best friends; we were never apart. "Wherever Sissy is, Bernie is," people used to say. "How would Sissy manage without Bernie?" The thought of functioning in a world without him was unfathomable. I was 60, and for the previous 30 years I'd been a wife, a mother, a busy volunteer. I was someone with a lot of energy, someone who could get things done. Then Bernie was gone, and I was blindsided. Suddenly even the simplest, everyday things became impossible to do. I couldn't set the clock, record my favorite show, continue my routine.

Gradually, though, I began to surface. I started to wear brighter clothing and jewelry. Close friends and acquaintances kept asking how I was coping so seemingly well. I didn't think I was doing anything different. I was just

trying to get through each day. Little by little, however, I began to ask myself if perhaps there was something that was helping me move forward.

I began to think that how I was coping had something to do with the way I approach life. I always simply ask myself: What will allow me to function best in a negative situation…what will make me the happiest? I know it sounds silly, but for me it works. But here's the important part: I trust that people will be there to help me and, just as importantly, I allow them to.

As I look back now, I worry I wasn't there for people who have gone through losing a partner. When I think of all those I know who have lost loved ones and what they have gone through, I realize I never understood; but now I know. Everyone is going to face death. And I want to be there for my family, my children, my friends and the community. It became my purpose to help others through their grief by sharing what I learned as I walked this walk. It became important for me to proclaim, "You can do it!"

For many years I have attended an annual authors' luncheon, and I would listen as writers said that everyone has a book in them. But it had never made a deep impression on me until my own life turned upside down. Yes— a book would allow me to tell people how I was coping.

I'd been a teacher, but writing a book was new territory for me. Where would I begin? I had an idea. During the four weeks when Bernie was ill and our daughters and I were at his side around the clock, Rabbi Steve Cohen, the new leader of Santa Barbara's Reform temple, Congregation B'nai B'rith, entered our lives. Steve was there offering support when Bernie was diagnosed; he was at Bernie's side when Bernie recited the *Sh'ma* (the most important Jewish prayer, which traditional Jews recite on rising and before sleep, and before death) and drew his last breath; and Steve presided over Bernie's memorial. Both before and after Bernie's death, he made me feel he was there for our family and for me. Rabbi Steve, with his tremendous spiritual depth and curiosity, could help to bring this book to life. He agreed to interview me and help draw out what I wanted to say.

By nature, Steve Cohen is an insightful questioner and a consummate listener. That was good fortune, because I love to talk! So he became part of the project. He would be my vehicle for healing, and it was our hope that my experience would give him a new path for learning. Despite all the demands on his time, he agreed to set aside an hour and a half weekly for us to meet. He thought that an ongoing conversation with a person willing to share her emotions and experiences honestly as she moved through the grieving process could help him to grow as a rabbi.

This book grew out of our seven months of weekly conversations that began five months after Bernie's funeral. They concluded at the first *yahrzeit* (anniversary of death).

Meeting over breakfast at the Breakwater restaurant, a small café in Santa Barbara's harbor, our conversations had no agenda. Many times I would bring a topic, sometimes Steve would initiate a topic, or we would just talk about something that had happened the previous week. He witnessed my baby steps, the first of everything I did. While he was always my rabbi, he also was part interviewer, part therapist and, ultimately, family. Although Steve and I are both Jewish, the book has a non-denominational approach to grieving—the loss of a partner is a universal experience.

Each of the conversations between Rabbi Steve and myself, and as well as several with friends and family, were taped, totaling more than 40 hours of cassettes. Then they were transcribed, turning into some 400 pages of nearly 100,000 words! Virtually everything you read here (with the exception of some bits added for clarity and continuity) comes from those transcripts. Even though it all came from discussions between Steve and me, most of it reflects just my side of the conversations. (If I didn't already know I loved to talk, reading the transcripts confirmed it!) To put the whole thing into book form, I entrusted it to my friend and next-door neighbor Laurie Deans Medjuck, a

B'nai B'rith congregant who is a writer and editor. She had suggested the interview process and taping of it in the first place, and when it was completed she edited and structured it into the book you are now reading.

On this journey I have learned that grief is a powerful teacher. It teaches you that you still have choices. You have a choice to accept the situation as graciously as possible and begin to author a new existence for yourself, or to lie down and die. It's not like anyone is going to escape the challenge. Losing loved ones is truly part of the cycle. How you respond is up to you—you can lock yourself up or you can use it as a vehicle to find yourself.

So I am doing what I set out to do: showing people that you can see the sunlight after a tragedy. It's not always going to be hazy and gray. The sun will shine again.

★

Throughout this book you will find quotations from my mother, Buddie Shrier. Some of these I found after she died, written on lists and pieces of paper and collected in a small wooden box. Others were simply things I heard her saying on an everyday basis. The life lessons they express formed the foundation of my life and had an enormous influence on how I coped as I mourned the loss of my husband.

Taking a Breath and Beginning the Journey...

"Stop holding your breath and counting the minutes until the pain is over."

—Anne Brener
Mourning and Mitzvah

1. Into the Cocoon

Grounding Myself in Safe Places

WE HAD just come back from Mexico, where we celebrated Bernie's 66th birthday on February 9, 2005. Bernie had a low fever, but he didn't think much of it. Our anniversary was April 10, and two weeks later he went in for medical tests. We found out on April 28 that there was something wrong: Bernie had a rare form of stomach cancer, and it had spread. That was the day my world stood still. It was a total, total shock. I fought like a wild woman, because I couldn't believe any of it.

Bernie died on June 1. I hadn't expected it would go that fast. I knew he was going to die, but I didn't know it would be so soon. Fewer than 24 hours after he came home from the hospital he took his last breath, surrounded by me and our daughters, and we held hands and said good-bye.

The memorial service several weeks later was more wonderful than I could have imagined. Hundreds of people came. Friends near and dear to Bernie and me took their turns speaking, recalling good times, their love of this wonderful man who had been such an indelible part of their lives. Rabbi Steve lauded Bernie's giving spirit, his enduring generosity in the community. I felt buoyed up by people's words, their love of Bernie, their embrace and support of me.

Afterwards was a blur. I recall concerned faces coming up to me and saying something nice about Bernie, asking how I was doing. I couldn't think how to answer them. I may have said, "Fine, and how are you?" But I wasn't really thinking. And then it was time to go home.

I don't think I noticed a single traffic signal or stop sign on that so-familiar route. But stepping through my front door I told myself I had to get in gear—I should call someone, I should take the trash out, water the yard.

From the moment Bernie became ill, I had recognized how important it was for me to keep it together. I was the one who still had to function. I had to keep the ship afloat. If I were to fall apart, that's what our children (then ages 26, 27 and 36) would see. They have long lives ahead, and I wanted them to know how to cope with adversity and survive. As soon as the memorial service was over, I wanted to get myself back into my usual "Sissy-mode." But I just couldn't. I sat down and didn't move. It was like I was in a fog.

I knew that feeling from when I buried my mother, and then my father. And then I remembered that I'd had my partner by my side during those times to help me through the loss. Who was going to help me get through this? How was I going to move on? I remembered my mother. She took care of herself. "I am *not* selfish," she proclaimed. "You can only take care of others if you take care of yourself first. People will come into your space; they will wear you down. This cannot be allowed—not by your husband, children or parents. Remember that you can only be as good to others as you are to yourself."

I took her words to heart and I decided I was not going to do anything for three months. I wanted just to be, and have my children with me. Friends, I felt, could wait—and thanks to the e-mails that my daughter Francine sent out, they understood. I had to heal in my own time in my own way.

A week after Bernie's death, Francine e-mailed this letter:

Dear Friends,

As we go through the greatest challenge in our lives, we want to thank you for the incredible love and support that we feel each and every day. The week of shiva was not a time of mourning, but a time of tribute. Thank you for celebrating Bernie with us. The stories and thoughts that you shared not only recognized his giving and doing ways, but inspired others to do the same. The Braille Institute has a new volunteer. The Fighting Back mentoring program may have a new "big sister."

Three hundred fifty people attended the funeral, and five hundred people attended the memorial service! Bernie was rich in friends and love. Thank you to CALM, our temple havurah, Hadassah and the B'nai B'rith Lodge for feeding the masses.

Today life is overwhelming. We spend our times doing "business." We go to banks, Social Security and the lawyer's office. We empty closets and fix household problems. We are learning to do all the things that Bernie did with such ease that we didn't even know he was doing anything at all.

This summer Sissy, Nadine and Franny will be living together. Next week is our annual family vacation. Bernie had planned a full week of fun in Santa Barbara. We will have a full house and a full week—Red Rock, the zoo, Land Shark tour, Morro

Bay.... It will undoubtedly be bittersweet. In August, Sissy will be stepping into Bernie's size 12 shoes and making the pilgrimage to Trinity, Texas, with Franny. By September Sissy will be home alone and hopefully ready to resume her active life. As for the summer, we will remain in our cocoon. Sissy will not participate in her organizations until September. Please forgive her for not returning phone calls and e-mails. Your love and prayers are helping us heal, but only time will do the trick.

With love, the Taran family

Now when I come home, it's to an empty house. I leave a light on, I have an alarm system, but still I open the door to that quiet. I'm there by myself. When I get up in the morning, I feel the quiet, but the morning is becoming a time for contemplation. And at the end of the day, I can't wait to get into my own bed and snuggle up. I actually have used only my side of the bed. I put pillows on his side so I don't roll over and I won't feel that empty space. It's like I'm in a little container, my little area, my little nest. And I'm snuggling up to myself. Living alone isn't what I'd call comfortable, but I'm working at it. I'm trying to accept the challenge of life, and hugging myself.

Many people have asked me when I am going to move. *"Move?"* I reply in shock. It is the very ground where I am living that is grounding me. I understand why some people,

people who have sad feelings in their homes (perhaps a spouse had a long illness there), want new surroundings or need to move for financial reasons. For me, my home is where I feel most comfortable. My home is my nest.

I have often gone to bed wondering why I love my house so much, what makes me feel so snug, so protected there. I've realized that the comfort of being in my home is that everything is familiar. I have "embracing objects"—a keepsake from a trip, art our children made, family photographs. Half of the possessions in my house came from my mother. My dining room set was my grandmother's. My father lived in the house for five years. Bernie and I had twelve wonderful years there. The house represents my family; it's where I feel everybody's presence.

But even in my fragile, beginning-to-heal condition, I knew I needed to find places other than my home where I could feel safe and comfortable.

Every Friday evening I went to Shabbat (Sabbath) services at our temple, and in the early days, unless my children were with me, I sat alone. Not that I wasn't invited to sit with people, but I needed that alone time, and people respected that. I did not attend the social after the services because it was too scary for me to interact with others. I would see people whom I hadn't seen in a while, and it was that touching and that look—I knew they really cared, but it was still painful for me. I didn't want to feel the discomfort when I had to answer the inevitable question about how I was doing. But at services was where my heart needed to be.

Another of my "safe places" was the bereavement group (under the auspices of the local hospice organization) where I went every other week for an hour and a half. I didn't know anyone, and there was total confidentiality. The meetings were about validating and sharing feelings, listening to other people's stories, hearing how they were handling the same things I was. I heard people talking about the same feelings I had, and I felt safe there with my feelings. We were all at the same place. It was in the bereavement group that I realized that it wasn't just me who would feel overwhelmed in the grocery store—too many choices on the shelf—and just flee, leaving the cart.

Participating in the bereavement group was a totally positive experience in spite of the fact that I heard such sad stories. It was during those meetings that I first became aware of my strength and knew that while helping myself I could help others.

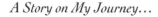

A Story on My Journey...
Breath Is Passage to the Soul

I discovered that the Hebrew word for "breath" and for "soul" is the same—*neshama*. Life begins with breath: God breathes our souls into our bodies. We often think that we're nurturing ourselves if we garden or walk or swim or journal or listen to our dreams. Somehow we forget that the very essence of nurturing ourselves—what truly makes us alive—is breathing. It doesn't get more basic than that. Shallow breathing cannot nourish the body.

One of the most important things I learned during the mourning process is about breathing. When we become familiar with our breath, and get to know our own particular rhythm, it can be a comfort to us. In times of tragedy we can learn how to use our breath to calm down.

I have a stone I bought at the hospital that says "Breathe." For months I would carry it, and it was my friend. I would take it in my hand to remind myself that when I became overwhelmed I was still in control of my breath. Now when something happens that sets me off, I just breathe in slowly and let it out. I pause and say, "I'm alive, I'm in control"—maybe not in control of my emotions at that moment, but that I can get in control. If I can be in control of breathing slowly in and slowly out, I can be in control of this. It takes me to a real place of nourishment.

"We, the Shriers, can't afford the luxury of depression."

—Buddie Shrier
(Sissy Taran's mother)

Life Lesson

I'm not saying I didn't cry in the grocery store. Or in yoga. I cried in both. But when I found my safe places—places where I didn't feel judged by people who didn't understand—I could be more comfortable with my emotions. I could begin to heal.

2. The Care and Maintenance of Me

When I Nurture Myself, the Healing Begins

I THINK even in a crisis you go to your strengths. My starting point in a negative situation has always been to ask myself what will make me the most comfortable, what will let me function best. Usually the answer is to organize—to try to gain some control. Right after Bernie's death, I divided my life into a half-dozen areas of concentration to help me try to move forward.

Emotional

If my house falls apart, I have a handyman. If my garden needs attention, I have a gardener. I'm just as important as the house and the garden, right? So I arranged to have a person—someone I admire—that I could call if I was falling apart or about to fall apart, or when I just needed to talk to somebody. I could just say to her, "I am having trouble," and that felt comforting.

I think you have to feel the pain, and go with it. I knew that if I didn't face the grief at the moment, I would most certainly face it later. In my bereavement group meetings I saw that many people would try to mask their pain with alcohol and drugs, but I realized that would only be a temporary distraction. I knew this awful period had to be experienced directly.

Health

I focused on eating, taking vitamins and sleeping. I've always taken my vitamins, so I continued to do that. Eating wasn't difficult. A schedule was set up with one of my friends making sure that I had food in the house, so I didn't have to go grocery shopping or cook. I just had to eat. Food would come in every three days.

People cannot function if they can't sleep, so sleep was one of the first things I zeroed in on. I needed to figure out how to sleep. I took sleeping pills and listened to meditation CDs. That worked. I took the pills for almost two months, but then I decided I had to figure out how to sleep on my own. I consulted a sleep expert (see the story "My Sleep Guru," page 42) and it helped. I didn't take another pill.

Mental

I failed at this part in the beginning. I'd wanted to play a hand of bridge a day but I couldn't do that for months. I thought this would help me focus, but it wasn't realistic at that time.

Exercise

I knew I had to get my body back into the mode of exercise, to get those endorphins going in order to sleep and function better. Going back to the gym was hard because I was afraid of talking with people, even though they were people I'd been exercising with for ten years. It took me about four or five times to get used to being back. By the fourth time I was there, people didn't say "Oh!" or hug me or touch my face and do all those things. While you're mourning you must still live in the present. You can't live in the past—it's too painful.

I returned to a mind–body class. I think that with the repetition of movements in yoga, tai chi or a mind–body

movement class where it's not competitive, you can start really focusing on the present, and being in the present is a gift. That repetition, week after week, was very comforting to me. It was a time when I could get into my head, into my spirit and into my body. I learned to go into myself. I wasn't looking at anyone else, not judging anyone else. It helped me understand who I am, and have patience with myself. Maybe the classes helped me accept a lot of my pain.

Safety

I had read that in the aftermath of a crisis you're not focused, and as a result you can be vulnerable. You could be in a car accident, have your house robbed, have a fall—all kinds of things. My own safety is important to me, so I tried to pay attention and focus. I had a check-off list and notes in my house to make sure that I was taking care of things. It said things like: "Did you get the mail? Did you lock the front door?"—reminders of the things I needed to do for my own safety. We'd never had an alarm system in the house, so I put one in (though I think it was partly to keep my friends from bugging me about getting one). I also had more sensor lights installed outside the house. I had extra house keys made, photocopied my credit cards, and kept a list of important phone numbers by my bed. I started using a smaller purse and sometimes a fanny pack.

I constantly reminded myself to avoid rushing and taking chances. I would always think to tell myself: think fast—move slow. I knocked on wood, took precautions, and I didn't have a catastrophe.

Spiritual

All those practical things took up much of my focus, especially in the early months, but looking after my spiritual health may have been the most important. As I said earlier, going to Friday night services at temple was a safe haven for me. It was a place where I could cry but, more importantly, it was a place that could help me heal. I felt I needed contact with God, and that's where I found it.

Another spiritual thing I did right from the beginning was continue being a mentor with the national Fighting Back program for at-risk children. Our young mentees, nine and ten at the time, had gone through Bernie's illness and passing; one of the children had spoken at the memorial. I felt that these children needed continued contact with me so, even though I didn't have contact with my friends, I kept up my hands-on involvement with them. I believe this commitment helped heal me. To know that I was continuing the work that Bernie and I had done together and that I was helping somebody else made a huge difference in my coming to terms with him not being here.

A Story on My Journey...

My Sleep Guru

I was using meditation tapes and taking sleeping pills, but I would still wake up in the middle of the night between two and four in the morning, angry that I was getting sleep-deprived. If I'm deprived of sleep, I can't function, and I get more and more terrorized about how I'm going to make it. So I went to Dr. Sue Colin to help with my sleep problem. Sue has a Ph.D. in counseling psychology and is a marriage and family therapist who runs the Holistic Counseling Center for Healing in Santa Barbara. She believes that in every tragedy there is a valuable lesson if you are willing to hear it. The more you avoid paying attention, the bigger the problem becomes. In order to be on the path of healing, one must embrace the problem. In one hour she completely changed how I approached sleeping.

The first thing Sue told me was to cover up the clock and not look at it. She said the worst thing I could do was look at it and get angry. So I just put a pillow in front of it.

Then she told me I was being awakened by something or somebody trying to reach me—my husband or another spirit—and that instead of worrying about not sleeping I should invite the spirit in and ask if he had something to say to me. I kind of laughed at this, because it's such a childish approach. But it worked. If I woke up, instead of being angry that I was up, I would ask, "Well, have you got something you want to say to me?" And if not, I would tell the spirit, "Well, I am going to go back to bed. I welcome you to come again when you need to."

The third thing Sue told me about was a progressive relaxation method, where you count backwards from ten to one, going deeper and deeper while systematically relaxing your body. You go through your whole body, tightening up everything and letting it go, always breathing deeply so you're not holding any tension. You start with your feet at "ten"— my feet are so heavy I can't move them; then "nine"—my calves are heavy and relaxed—all the way through your hips, and shoulders and arms—to "one," your head.

Sue also told me I could program myself to dream before I went to sleep, and to tell my unconscious mind to let my conscious mind know my dream in the morning. She said that if I woke up with thoughts, to write them down but not try to make any sense out of them. Later I might see something in them.

Lastly, she recommended not eating two hours before going to bed and not drinking alcohol. She suggested not watching television, particularly the news. If I had to watch something, I should make it something soothing, like a nature program.

Life Lesson

How does one start to cope again with life? I think it's possible because of the experiences that are inside you. Somehow, if you allow yourself—and *allow* is really an important word—to believe that you're still important because you're still alive, something comes forward. I cannot cry for 24 hours. It won't happen. There are days that I might be sad for, say, 23 hours, but I had some consciousness for at least a short time to begin with. Gradually the time got longer. What I needed to do to take care of myself began to get clearer in my head. Then, when I began to nurture myself, I believe the healing began to happen.

3. If You Don't Ask, You Can't Receive

Being Open and Reaching Out Is Key

IN THOSE first few months when I found myself in any new situation, whether it was dealing with a doctor, a credit card company, the cable company or the bank, the first words out of my mouth were, "My husband just passed away. I've never done this. Be patient, talk slowly, and don't yell at me." When I announced right up front that I didn't know how to do something and explained my situation, people were gentle and went out of their way to help me.

I quickly discovered it was okay to let people know I could use their help. And that didn't mean just my inner circle of friends. It included my gardener, my handyman, my bank manager, my neighbors. I found it was good to surround myself with people who were aware of my situation and who cared. I feel that I put together a team of caring people who were helping me function in my world.

Moreover, I believe that people *wanted* me to tell them how they could help. After the memorial I realized it wasn't just me and the children who were in mourning—our friends were grieving too. The first thing many said was, "What can I do?" If I didn't have an answer, they would feel helpless. When I could suggest something, it made them feel needed and they could better cope with the loss. If I didn't know what to answer when friends asked, I'd give them the name of a person to call—"Call Joan, she's in charge of the food"—and that took it out of my personal responsibility. The best part was that it made people feel like they were needed—and of course they were.

It's how I've operated in fund-raising and philanthropic work. I've been in volunteer work for all my adult life, and often chaired committees. I am used to calling people up and asking them to do things. Generally, if I say I need help, people will help. But I know I have to reach out. I truly believe in my heart that if I ask somebody I'm giving that person the opportunity to do a *mitzvah* (good deed) and to feel good about himself or herself. When I allow someone to help, I think that person's life is enriched as well as mine.

Life is complicated, and because losing a partner is going to happen to many of us, I think everybody needs a support system. Naturally, it's easier to call a team into action if you have a team in place before a crisis. My friends have always been an important part of my life, and when Bernie died the circle enlarged. I didn't want to lean too much on my kids—they were also in much pain.

A few friends have disappointed me. The majority have surprised me with their tremendous support; they've come to my aid every time I picked up the phone. Even though it was difficult for some people—those who don't reach out very often—they too stepped up. That's the gold at the end of the rainbow.

"The only thing that starts big is grief. It is also the only thing that grows smaller as the days pass."

—Buddie Shrier

21st Century Blues

Ten days after Bernie died, I went to the bank to get money out. The teller told me I needed to use an ATM card. I just started to cry and said, "I don't know how." I was 60 years old and I'd never used an ATM! I explained my situation, and the bank manager came out and showed me the process. She gave me a hug and said she missed my husband. It really made me feel good that she had wonderful memories of him.

When I went to my physical therapist, the office assistant told me I hadn't reached my deductible and I owed money. I burst into tears and said, "I'll pay you whatever you want me to pay you. I've never done this before. My husband just died." It was all new to me because Bernie had always paid the bills.

When I tried to cancel Bernie's cell phone, the company rep told me I couldn't because we had a four-year contract. I said, "But he's dead. What can I do? My husband died and isn't using this telephone!" I was at a loss, but I asked to speak to the supervisor. Once again I explained the problem. This time I was understood and I got action: Bernie's phone was cancelled, and I was kept on the same plan. The supervisor told me what troubles his mother was having, and said he understood what I was going through. I discovered again that my openness helped me.

"Forward ever, backward never!"
—Buddie Shrier

Life Lesson

I've learned there's no point in being a martyr. People want to be asked to help and lend support. People are fundamentally caring; they will very seldom turn you down. I think the most important thing is to open up and reach out, to open yourself up to trust and allow people to be there to help you. Making the moves—that's crucial. If you are open, you can receive; you can't receive if you're not available to receive. That's the secret.

4. My Good Friend the Calendar

Structuring My Days

BERNIE used to say that my birthday wouldn't be over before I was planning my next one. And it's true. I always want to have something to look forward to, even more now than I used to. I find myself planning ahead for everything because I try not to have times when I could be lonely and depressed. (I am fortunate that I didn't need to suddenly get a job when my husband died, but that meant that there would be less structure in my life.)

I don't want to "let come what may." If you have a "hole" that needs to be filled, don't expect other people to fill it! You're in charge of your own holes, your own destiny. Planning ahead is now a priority for me.

Everyone has a good friend, one who is dependable and won't let you down in your hour of need. Well, mine happens to be my calendar—make that *calendars*. In fact, I have four calendars, each with different purposes:

1. Pocket/purse: doctor appointments, personal care

2. Desk/master: meetings, invitations, plus the above

3. Sissy's week-at-a-glance (see next page): 1 day-by-day sheet, to carry

4. One-year wall calendar: trips and vacations

I want to describe the method I use to be organized. At the end of each week, I plan out every day of the coming week using calendars 2 and 3. I look to see where I have holes, and then I make sure to fill the holes. I don't want to leave myself open to the sadness that could come from too much empty time, so I line up things to do. For example, one Sunday when I saw that I had nothing to do I called a neighbor and said, "I have a DVD at my house—want to come have popcorn and watch?" I've got to have plans, and I don't like to leave things to the last minute. This type of organization helped me to begin focusing on each day.

Just like I can't function without planning ahead, I can't function without structure and order in my day. I like knowing what I did yesterday and what I'm doing today

Sissy's weekly calendar

"Wishing you a good day today,
and a better day tomorrow!"
— Buddie Shrier

and tomorrow. I find a lot of comfort in routine. After
three months, I resumed going to meetings, playing cards,
tutoring at school—all of my old routines. At the outset,
I put together a daily chart showing everything I wanted
or needed to do. I called it my "star system." It was something familiar to me because I had used a similar system
when I taught school and also when raising the children.
It had rows for activities I wanted to accomplish on a daily
basis. I'd put a check mark in the box next to each item I
completed that day. I usually got about half done. Then at
the end of the week I would reward myself with a gift—a

Star System	7/5	6	7	8	9	10	11	12	13	14
sit down to eat	✓	✓	✓	✓		✓	✓	✓		
read paper	✓	✓	✓		✓		✓	✓		✓
do a bridge hand										
foot and leg exercises	✓	✓	✓					✓	✓	
10,000 steps (pedometer)					✓	✓			✓	
write thank you notes	10	12				5	5			
deal with people					✓	✓		✓		
do good deeds					✓					
no sugar	✓					✓				
take vitamins	✓	✓	✓	✓	✓	✓	✓	✓	✓	

Sissy's motivational chart

ceramic frog. And that is how I started my outdoor frog collection! After four weeks of this kind of discipline and four frogs, I abandoned the system. It had worked, and I no longer needed the motivation.

I knew that just as there were essential things I had to do (such as brushing my teeth, taking a bath, eating, understanding finances), there were also things that I didn't have to do, or things that didn't need to be done by me. Those I either dropped or asked a friend to be in charge of, so I wasn't bombarded by what I didn't have to deal with.

Life Lesson

Even if it was just following the footsteps of the day before, I found that it was routine and structure that helped me get through the days. Plotting everything in my calendars kept me on track and brought a sense of order to the chaos of my internal world. It gave me something to hold on to, and warned me what was coming up or if I would have too much time on my hands. For me, looking ahead and having plans means I am alive and going forward.

Making Friends with the New Normal...

"Change is upsetting.
Repetition is tedious.
Three cheers for variation!"

—Mason Cooley,
City Aphorisms

5. The First of Everything Is Really Hard

...And the Holidays Are Hardest of All

WE WANT things to be as they were, what "normal" was. We say, "It shouldn't be this way, I want it the other way." At the bereavement group I heard again and again, "It's not fair, we shouldn't be here." But ultimately we knew that it didn't matter if it was fair; it's as it is. When we ended our meetings and held hands the group chanted, "And so it is."

I have never been comfortable with change, but now the big change of being on my own has become my "new normal." I may not want to take out the trash, do the finances or make sure I'm secure in my house, but I have to do these things; there's no one else to do them. But instead of fighting it, I am trying to accept it.

When it came to the first holidays, I knew they wouldn't be easy. I knew they would be difficult, but I didn't think they were going to be as hard as they were. When the season began, every single day brought a new wave that would just crash over me. I felt miserable, even though people were trying to help me not feel bad.

The whole period from Thanksgiving to New Year made me profoundly sad. Everywhere I'd go I'd see everybody smiling at one another. I felt bombarded by happiness and cheer that I couldn't share in. I have boxes and boxes of decorations for every holiday—I couldn't open one of them. I would start to remember the joy of bringing everyone together and celebrating. I remembered how we'd chronicle every celebration with photographs. I thought about how difficult it would be to take pictures that Bernie wouldn't be in.

And so I just decided to have those first holidays without taking pictures. That decision allowed me to recognize that with holidays and celebrations it's important to do what's comfortable for me. That might mean doing what I always did, or changing it. I didn't have to do what I'd always done.

When it came to my birthday I knew I didn't want to celebrate it with my family, because it would be too painful. I believe people can substitute for other people, so I called my childhood girlfriend and I said, "Can I come to your house?" "Absolutely yes!" she replied. We went line dancing and "two-stepping" to country music, and I watched all the people in their funny outfits and crazy hairdos, and I did a lot of laughing. Nobody there knew me, so it was easier. I went back to childhood memories and my inner me. On the most important day of the year, I overcame fear and began reinventing my new adult self.

I also realized that I can't expect others to anticipate my needs. I've often heard people say, "They know I'm alone, why don't they call me? They should invite me." And I think, "No, *you* should invite *them*." If my kids couldn't be with me, I decided I wouldn't wait to be invited to somebody else's house. I'd make an event at *my* house. I'd think of somebody else who was alone and invite that person. It wouldn't even be important to cook. We could potluck it.

On Valentine's Day I wanted my married friends to know that I was happy for them. I didn't want them to feel like they couldn't tell me their plans. (Nevertheless they didn't, as though they might protect me from feeling bad.) But I had my own plans. I spent the day with my grandson, Ethan. We had a little cupcake party. Then Ethan, my daughter Tiffany and her husband, Scott, and I went out to dinner. My idea had been that I would baby-sit for my

daughter and son-in-law so they could go out. But we all ended up going out together, and that was really special. Next year, though, I plan to have a Valentine's Day Pajama Tea Party—women only.

The important thing for me on all such occasions is to have a plan, just like I have an emergency earthquake plan. I always want to be prepared before I find the ground shaking under me!

"Of all human emotions, self-pity is the most ridiculous."

—Buddie Shrier

A Story on My Journey…
Good Things, Bad Things

The first major holiday that came up was Thanksgiving, and I knew I wasn't emotionally ready to orchestrate a big family gathering at my home as I had done every year for as long as I could remember. Instead we had it with my eldest daughter and her family. After that, I realized I wasn't ready to let it go. I had been lonely, but not just for my husband. I was also lonely for my holiday. I think of Thanksgiving as *my* holiday, maybe because it falls near my birthday, and I always make a big deal out of it. I decided to take it back the next year.

When it came to celebrating Hanukkah, Christmas and New Year, which I am not as personally attached to, I still didn't want to deal with the memories I'd have at home. I spent New Year in Palm Springs with Tiffany, Scott and my grandson. We have a family tradition. At every gathering we go around the table and each person is asked to state one good thing and one bad thing that has happened. That New Year's Eve we had all been avoiding saying that Bernie had died. Then it was my almost-four-year-old grandson's turn. He said the bad thing was that "Papa Bernie isn't here." And with his innocence of "Papa Bernie isn't here" it was okay to say it. It was the bad thing. But we were all there together, and that was the good thing.

Life Lesson

No one says getting through the holidays is a piece of cake, so I wanted to make plans that would protect me and cause me the least amount of discomfort. I thought it would be a mistake if I tried to recreate what I had done before, so I chose different locations and different forms of celebration. I found that lessened the pain. With preparation, I found I could manage the holidays. And maybe even celebrate a little.

6. Two Steps Forward, One Step Back

There's No Choice But to Ride the Wave

I'D BEEN exercising at the "Y" for more than 10 years, and two months after the funeral I went back. The regimentation and routine had always been a tremendous comfort to me. Before a class I would do circuit training and weights and not socialize with anybody. It was quiet, I could get into my head, into my spirit and into my body. I remember one time in a jazz dance class when a particularly moving song came on and I started to cry. The tears were rolling down my cheeks. The instructor quietly went over to the CD player, ejected that CD and replaced it with another. Not a word was spoken, not a beat dropped, and I continued the class feeling embraced by the teacher.

It took very little to trigger that big wave of emotion. I realized that I might go forward two steps one day, and the next day I might go back a step. Sometimes it seemed I was ahead of the game, and other times it seemed that six months earlier I'd been in better shape. Some days I didn't think I was ever going to move on. But I have learned in the past year that grieving is a process of waves. It is not a smooth, chronological course.

Sometimes I've been emotionally raw, but I believe that if I were to hold back that wailing and that tremendous pain, I wouldn't grow or be able to handle the next wave that inevitably is coming. I couldn't worry about making a fool of myself or making other people feel uncomfortable. I just had to let myself grieve. Of course I didn't want to let it out on a glorious occasion like a wedding, because I didn't want to put a damper on things when others were celebrating. (But of course, if you're crying at a wedding, nobody will wonder why.) I know that the waves can come any time—usually when least expected. Knowing that gives me permission to be comfortable with my emotions.

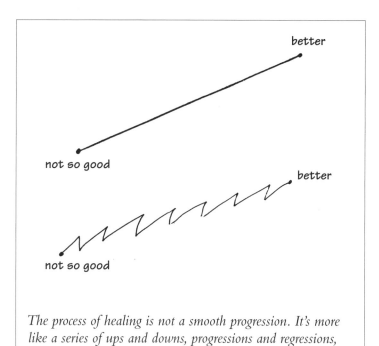

better

not so good

better

not so good

The process of healing is not a smooth progression. It's more like a series of ups and downs, progressions and regressions, leaps and backslides.

"Let the tears flow and flow."
—Buddie Shrier

My Coming Out Party

For the first three months I consciously avoided situations in which I would be emotionally vulnerable, especially social events with couples. The first such event I attended—my "coming out party"—was a celebration with about 250 people at my temple that didn't feel "couple-ish." I wanted to be prepared, so I arranged to have friends pick me up and to have someone there to hold my hand if I became uncomfortable. I thought I was prepared for the evening.

I walked in and said hello to the greeters at the door. Then I saw people I hadn't seen in a while, and it was that touching and that look, and the first thing they said to me was "How are you?" They didn't say it the way they used to say it. Actually, they may have said it like they used to say it—I just heard it differently. I heard it said with a sad puppy dog expression, and that unhinged me a bit. But I managed, until I walked into the crowded silent auction. Suddenly I couldn't breathe, I think because Bernie's favorite thing had been silent auctions—I hadn't even remembered until then. I had a panic attack like you wouldn't believe. I, who had so much confidence in my little box of tricks, who thought, "Oh, great, I can handle this…." I have to tell you, sometimes the wrench doesn't quite work with the nut and the bolt, or the screwdriver doesn't quite go into the top of the screw.

My friends got me a drink, and I was appreciative that they were aware of what was happening. But I could not get control. I left the room and went to the check-in table, and sat down next to a woman I know. She looked at me, then just held me while I wailed in her arms like a three-year-old until the friend who was going to hold my hand found me and took me to a quiet room where I could catch my breath.

I finally got myself together and took a seat in the very back of the social hall for the dinner, with a friend on each side. It was still rough. Everyone was celebrating and honoring people, and part of me was saying, "Isn't this wonderful?" and wanting to participate. But another part was saying, "How come they're holding hands?—I'll never be able to do that." Then I heard the DJ tell all the men to take their women to the dance floor, and I was so upset and so angry I couldn't have my person. On a very happy, joyous occasion I was bombarded by waves of sadness.

I guess I was naïve. I'd thought that because I'd be at the same place and with many of the same people I saw on Friday nights (when I help prepare and serve the monthly community dinner), it wouldn't be hard. But those nights are different. I am busy running around serving people. I'm

not somebody others have pity for. Suddenly my safe temple wasn't so safe. And even though I'd come armed with my tools—my friends, a plan of action—I went all the way down.

Eventually I joined in the dancing, including some really fast dancing with friends—women and men—and it was okay. I danced and danced and let those endorphins come out. I did not sit at the table and feel sorry for myself. I got through the entire evening.

"Even when I can't see the sun I know that it's there."

—Buddie Shrier

Life Lesson

I've learned that you have to ride the wave. There's nothing else you can do, because the wave is going to keep coming, and you've got to breathe through it and get to the end and know you'll be plunked down again and again. But it's good to know that these things happen and that you can go all the way down and still come back up.

7. The Buck Stops Here

Making My Own Decisions

BERNIE AND I definitely had our roles in our family. While I was busy working on committees and fund-raisers, he was at home making all the decisions and looking after everything. I did not take my car in to be serviced. I did not balance the bank account. I did not pay the bills. I never made an airline reservation. He would say, "You've got e-mails," and he would have gotten rid of all the spam. From the time we married, he handled all of that. He wanted to, and I was happy to let him.

Then all of a sudden I was coming home to all this stuff—all of the junk e-mails, whether the doctor charged too much, if the car needed servicing.... When I first looked at all the things I had to decide about, I was so afraid. Could I handle "his" jobs?

Now, for the first time in my life, I am making all the decisions. I have to make decisions about myself, the children, the house and the finances. I no longer have a mother or a father or a husband to rely on. Truly the buck stops here. At first it's scary, but then a kind of pride develops. I am starting to fill myself up with my own confidence of "Gee, you did that."

I could have become depressed because I was suddenly weighed down by all these new responsibilities. But my new perspective is: These are my responsibilities, and I choose to accept them.

I have become more comfortable doing things for myself, and deciding to delegate others. In areas where I've needed help (such as security and finance) I've brought in people to help me, not necessarily the people I would have normally reached out to—not just my best friends, not just my inner circle—but people I simply believe are competent to give me advice. For me that is a very different approach.

I do reflect back to Bernie's decisions constantly, and sometimes I use his thinking. I took the car in to get it repaired the way he would do it. However, I have devised my own filing system. I also decided to water the plants more. (Of course, I did get a much higher water bill, but that was my choice.) Still, I've realized that when I do the

finances, I always do it late at night, in the office, at his
desk. I feel I'm channeling him! I do it like he did, I think,
to feel closer to him—it's very comforting to me. So far, I
feel I've made good decisions, which makes me feel better,
and makes me think he's there watching me.

"You are never in the soup, under a cloud,
up a creek, over a barrel, down the drain,
out on a limb or off your rocker."
—Buddie Shrier

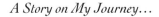

A Story on My Journey…

The New Driveway

For twelve years, ever since we bought our house, Bernie and I had discussed over and over how we could change the circular driveway that we'd never liked. But we couldn't figure out how to do it and afford it. The asphalt was getting worse and worse, and I was driving up to the house every day and seeing ugly. I didn't want to see ugly anymore, so I decided to put in a new driveway. This was really a present to myself, but I decided I wanted to have it done by Bernie's birthday, as kind of a present to him too.

I talked to a neighbor who had redone his driveway, and he brought over a contractor who made a proposal I liked. I asked him to write up a contract, but he said, "No, we just shake hands." I got really nervous and asked my neighbor if this was okay. He said, "Yes, you just shake hands." I did and went ahead with the project.

Previously, when I'd needed to make a major decision, like finding a financial planner (a three-month process of research and interviewing people), I'd involved my attorney and a daughter, and we'd discussed the pros and cons at length. The driveway, my first major independent decision, was sort of biting the bullet. I felt it was a wise decision, because to spend money on my home was an investment as well as something that would give me pleasure. I didn't spend it on jewelry or travel. It was something concrete, and something that I would see every day and have fun developing.

When workers started tearing up the old driveway, I thought to myself, "You made a decision, and you made a decision that was for you." When it was completed and the plants I'd selected had been put in, it changed the whole look of the front of the house. The change was so beautiful I knew Bernie would love it. The positive feedback I heard from everybody felt good. I was so proud of myself that I had come up with it, that I did it and went through with it. I had accomplished something on my own.

"If you try to please everyone, you end up pleasing no one."

—*Buddie Shrier*

Life Lesson

Having to make decisions about things I'd never had to deal with is part of my personal growth. While I'm taking on this new role I'm finding a new me, and that's exciting. Rather than sitting at home and saying, "Oh, my God, how can I do this?" I'm beginning to really find some pride and strength in areas where I didn't know I had any (though the computer will never be one of them). And if I can't do it myself, at least I am getting smart enough to have everyone's phone number. I am really learning how to depend upon myself for the first time in my whole life.

8. Living with Zest

I Lost My Partner,
But I Didn't Lose My Purpose

I WAS FINDING it so hard to prepare dinner just for myself. One potato in the microwave just looked so lonely. Cooking was getting so depressing. But not long after Bernie's memorial, my temple started to put on monthly community dinners, and they asked for people to help prepare the meals. I didn't know anything about cooking for large groups, but I volunteered. Now I cook for up to 150 people once a month. I rush around like a crazy person, laugh a lot and get all kinds of accolades, but the best thing is the happiness it brings to many people. Cooking alone I dreaded, but cooking for a group I discovered is a purposeful and enjoyable experience. Finding new activities has helped me shed the loneliness.

I like to push outside the box. This is the time for experimentation, so I have decided to experiment. If I can't do it now, when will I ever be able to do it?

The entire time I was married I never traveled without my husband. I've taken two trips now—one with a girlfriend on a cruise around the British Isles, the other with family to South America. I challenged myself to make the plans and execute them, and they were big wows for me. Before I would never have said taking a trip was "a big wow," but now it's a big thing because it means I am doing something as an individual.

I've been painting, not by myself but at a friend's house, making greeting cards so I can give something of myself to friends. I decided to take yoga lessons—I had never done yoga. I love seeing movies and discussing them, but I don't always want the burden of making a date for the cinema. So, recently I've been watching DVDs at my house and inviting people over, and we talk about the movies over popcorn. Arranging movies at my house seems emotionally easier than the spontaneity of suggesting to someone that we go see a movie that night.

I decided to have an untraditional tea party—a pajama tea party, from 9 to 11 in the morning. Women only, women with whom I hadn't had a relationship as part of a couple. The invitation said, "Roll out of bed and join me for a pajama tea party. Pajamas required, makeup optional." A few were too embarrassed and wore sweats; some came like they actually just crawled out of bed; others bought brand-new pajamas because they couldn't be seen in their old pajamas. I had fifteen women in their pajamas, and it was a hoot because their personalities really showed. I made breakfast, people relaxed and talked, everyone loved it. I decided I am going to have three parties a year—a summer, a winter and a "whatever" party.

I love Scrabble, and I have found two people who like to play and we have a monthly Scrabble night. I also formed a group called "Go Goddesses"—six women and me. It's actually a spiritual kind of truth and finding-out-who-you-are gang, with people that I didn't know well.

I've found it's good to have people in my life other than just those who knew me as someone's partner, who know me as a widow. For instance, I have a friend who's a chef at a restaurant, and for fun I tried being a hostess there. I could talk to the guests and nobody knew me, nobody cared who I was. They didn't know what baggage I might carry. I did it and it was fun. Another step forward.

I can't recreate the bond that Bernie and I had. But I'm surrounding myself with new activities, new groups, new people, and developing new bonds.

Trips, yoga, movies and getting together with friends

are all enriching activities. But I know it's important not just to do things to fill my time, but to do things that will give my life meaning. If I want to feel better, I should help somebody else. There are times when I cannot find help, but I know there is no time when I cannot give help to another. There are so many people who need help, and so many programs (mentor programs, big sister and big brother programs, etc.) that need volunteers. Helping others, I know, can help heal me. I think if I were on my own just with my sadness, without helping someone else, it would be a much tougher path. I feel that if I were to focus only on myself and my sadness, then I would not be true to myself and what my commitment to life is all about.

"You find happiness by giving it."
—Buddie Shrier

Shall We Dance?

My grandson (who says the things that nobody else wants to say) was drawing a picture of a flower, and he told me, "This flower is for Papa." I replied, "What a beautiful flower!" And he said, "Grandma, you need a new Papa!" I said, "I don't know if I want a new Papa. I collect frogs in the garden, so can't I just get a new frog?" He said, "Oh, yes, you can get a new frog." "Is that just as good?" I asked. He said, "Yes, that's just as good."

I still want to dance, I still want to go out to socialize. I don't want to sit at a widow's table by myself. After Bernie died, I was afraid that our old friends would not want me in their lives, that I'd be a burden, somebody they found too needy. I didn't know anybody who was single; I knew only couples. I needed to figure out how to be included socially with both husbands and wives of our old friends. So I sort of reprogrammed my mind: I wouldn't be the third wheel—I would become part of a "*ménage à trois*." During a big celebration at my temple I had a "*ménage à trois* dance" with Rabbi Steve and his wife, Marian. I was so comfortable being welcomed into their arms.

Another time I was at a wedding, and I went up to a half-dozen men I knew and asked, "Can I put you on

my dance card?" and they said "yes." So I just went up to them when I needed a dance. If I was worried I might be uncomfortable at an event, I would ask a couple if they'd be there to hold my hand if needed. The couples felt that they were helping me, and I was so open about it that the women weren't jealous or afraid of me.

I can't do this with everybody, though. Some of my closest women friends find it difficult for me to join them and their husbands. They'll say, "Let's just the two of us girls have lunch." So I only can do it with the people who feel comfortable with me, with whom I feel comfortable, and then it works.

Nobody has dropped me. Nobody has not wanted to be there to help me. People say, "Anytime you want to have dinner, come over." I haven't stood on ceremony. Instead of waiting for people to ask me, I will ask, "Can I come over tonight?" I am included.

"Life may not be the party we hoped for, but while we are here we might as well dance."
— *Buddie Shrier*

Life Lesson

When I "step out of the box," just the mere stepping out is a brave step. It's taking a risk. It doesn't matter if I succeed. Taking the risk is the powerful action, whether anybody else knows about it or not. When I do it, I must be proud of myself.

I've always thought, if you're going to live, don't just exist. Step out of the box, get up with your tambourine and dance, because that's what we're here to do—to celebrate life!

9. You Can Huff and Puff, But You Can't Blow My House Down!

I Am a Powerful Human Being

MY HUSBAND used to fight all my battles for me. Problems with bills, plumbers, gardeners, he'd look after them. He'd even return my shoes to the department store! I believed I just didn't have the confrontational gene necessary for such encounters, or that if I tried I'd be intimidated and wouldn't get what I wanted, so I was grateful to have him do it for me.

When I was first on my own and faced with a situation that might involve confrontation, I'd simply avoid dealing with it. I'd pay the bills when they came in—no questions asked. Even when I would have preferred to have a written contract on the driveway project, I went along with the contractor's "just a handshake."

But then something changed. Perhaps it was my shoulder surgery and the bills that followed, or the charge for repairing the leak in my car's power steering, or the unforeseen costs with the driveway. I suddenly knew I didn't want to have either my money or my time wasted.

In a completely out-of-character move, I called the medical office and asked for an explanation of my statement and why they hadn't billed my insurance. I wasn't argumentative, I wasn't belligerent. And guess what? I got a "cash discount." I asked the mechanic to itemize the potential repairs on my car. He looked at me with respect. No one got mad, and I got what I wanted.

More importantly, I've realized that I *can* assert myself. And I don't have to be defensive or confrontational. I can simply state my concerns and ask what action can be taken. It doesn't get personal. It's just what any self-respecting businessperson—make that any self-respecting person—would do. It's empowering.

Now I remind myself: What's the worst thing anyone can do to me if I stand up for myself and ask for something? They can simply say "no"! And after you've been through the worst, that's nothing.

A Story on My Journey…

Not a House of Straw

When the workers demolished the driveway, the sink backed up in the kitchen. Under normal circumstances I wouldn't go berserk. But I panicked a bit because I had the young children I mentor at my house after an outing, and we were making pizzas and I had to get them home. I thought that the driveway demolition had caused it, and that my whole house might back up, and I was afraid to flush the toilets. So I called one of the rooter companies and they said they'd be there in an hour. I thought I was using my head.

Master Rooter (not the company's real name) sent someone. He came late, looked outside for the cleanout access, and said, "What idiot stuccoed over the cleanout hole?" He decided to go through the drain of the kitchen sink. He put his rooter in and black guck got everywhere, and I mean everywhere. He did it a second time and I had a mess. Then he announced that it didn't work. I was thinking, "I paid $170 for this?" He told me he'd have to do the next process—"swishing"—which would cost $300. I told him to come back first thing the next day. I arranged for someone to take the kids home and dashed to my bridge lesson (where I didn't do too well because I was thinking

about Master Rooter). Then I called my contractor friend who had redone my kitchen, explained the situation, and he said he'd come by first thing in the morning.

He arrived early and discovered the cleanout wasn't stuccoed over, but then he had to leave. At 9:00 A.M. five women arrived to do tai chi in my living room, and Master Rooter was late again. Finally two men showed up to do the swishing process. I told them I would like them to go in from the main opening because it's not stuccoed over, but the man who was there the day before said he wouldn't do it, he'd already done it twice through the sink. I said, "Just do me a favor, just satisfy me," but he refused. "I am sure it is a waste of time," I continued, "but it's my house and I would really like you to go in through the cleanout hole." He called his boss and told him, "This woman is throwing banana peels, grease, everything in the sink." I looked at him, and I was thinking, "I should be in the other room doing tai chi and grounding myself with Mother Earth. Instead I am arguing with this guy who is not telling the truth, who doesn't know that I have not even cooked for eight months!"

When he hung up, I gave him my credit card and told him to charge me just for yesterday, and I said I would call someone else to go in through the main cleanout because he'd been there for 20 minutes arguing with me and telling his boss lies. He called his boss again and said how impossible I was, and this time his boss told him to go in where I wanted them to go in, through the main cleanout.

I went into tai chi and, son of a gun, I heard the water going right down the drain. I didn't say a word. I was so proud. I didn't say, "I told you so." The rooter man agreed it was clear, but he still wanted to get the best of me. He said that if he didn't do the expensive swishing treatment it would clog up again in a couple of weeks and he'd have to come back.

This cocky young man was arguing with me because he wanted to get the best of me, but I had already won. He didn't like that. "Just charge me the $170," I said, "and if it clogs up again I will call you." I will never call that company again.

Six months ago I would have just melted into the ground. But this time I didn't, and I didn't scream or holler, and I got through it. I was really proud of myself.

I am much more careful now because Bernie is not there to bail me out or fight for me. Now I'm learning important skills for living independently. It's my house—I'm going to win. I'm not going to be blown down by any big bad wolf—or anybody else.

Life Lesson

Even though my partner is not here with me, he is here. Even though I don't have the physical presence of my loved ones who have passed on, they didn't take the strength they gave me with them. I can harness that strength to carry on. It can empower me. And as I take on new responsibilities and believe that I'm capable, those experiences empower me more. Look at what I can accomplish!

Bernie and Sissy, 2004.

Sissy with the "memory bench" she created to honor her family.

Close-up and detail of the "memory bench."

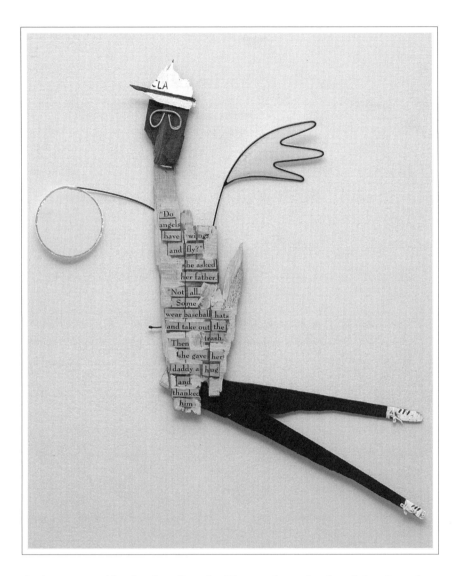

Sculpture created by daughter Francine Taran to honor her late father. It reads: "'Do angels have wings and fly?' she asked her father. 'Not all. Some wear baseball hats and take out the trash.' Then she gave her daddy a hug and thanked him."

Francine first created a sculpture for Sissy. It reads: "The woman with wild hair sat her children down and showed them the box that held her secrets to happiness. LOVE. Laughter. Lots of hairspray."

Bernie with Michael Lopez, whom he mentored with the Fighting Back pro-
gram, 2004.

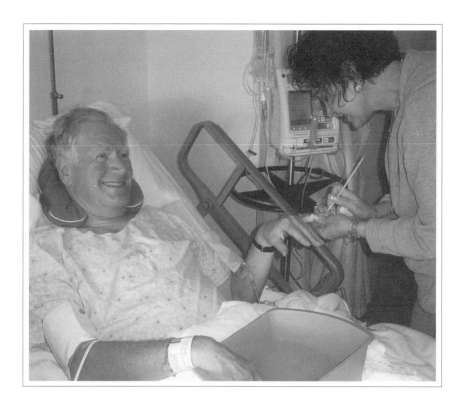

Bernie receiving a manicure from Sissy in the hospital three weeks before his death.

Sissy's daughters Tiffany, Nadine and Francine (left to right), sons-in-law Scott and Zach, and grandson Ethan at the wedding of Zach and Nadine, June 2006.

Oil portrait by Morris Squire.

Looking Back, Moving Forward…

"In our present, our future and our past are ours. It is by accepting your past, and by uniting the values and ideals of your marriage with your present, that you can find your future. And when at last you step whole into that future, you will know that the best of your marriage is within you and will always be there when you need it."

—Paul Tillich
The Eternal Now

10. Building on the Memories

My Version of Scrapbooking

I HAVE ALWAYS liked to surround myself with treasured things that bring me comfort—mementoes from trips, little things given to me by my parents and grandparents. All have tremendous value to me. I even wear clothes that once were worn by my mother, my father and Bernie because I have such fond memories of those people when I wear them. I guess you could say I'm sentimental. The past has always been an important part of my present, but I don't ever want to feel I'm stuck in the past.

Some people are romantic and always buy cards. Bernie was not. He would often forget Valentine's Day and our anniversary, so I had a card file in which I had saved all his cards from over the years. I would tell him, "Tomorrow is my birthday—get me a card." Or, "Tomorrow is Valentine's Day—get me a card." He just went to the file, pulled out one of the old cards, put a new date on it, and said, "This was always my favorite card." When my first Mother's Day without him came along, I looked at all the cards he'd given me, pulled one out and put it up. It said, "You warm my heart with affection." That was so nice. I thanked him. It was like his present to me.

On my first wedding anniversary without him I asked myself, "What do I miss the most?" I was missing the normal stuff—my husband to hug me, go to bed with, shop with, eat with. I planned a day I could get through, in which I could protect myself, that would be as pleasant a day as possible. I started with tai chi in the morning, then had lunch with two close friends, played bridge, and went to my weekly bereavement group. I received telephone calls from family all day long making sure that I was okay. I was definitely okay.

A friend invited me over for dinner where Bernie's poker group was meeting. That was the first time since his death that I had seen the guys together. They were as surprised to see me as I was to see them. They kibbitzed with me, and I listened in on their game. I realized how much I missed that.

Bernie and I would have been married 29 years. I'm not marking it that way anymore. That would have been about the old me. I have a new counting system to mark it. When June 1, the day of his death, comes, that will be a one-year anniversary for me. Not that he died a year ago, but that I lived for a year, and I'm going to live another, and another. Maybe no one else will ever think of it that way, but I'll be celebrating. Anniversaries are going to be like birthdays for me. And I'm going to do things to celebrate.

A Story on My Journey…

The Memory Bench

I redesigned the driveway in front of my house to replace asphalt with landscaping. My thought was that every time I drove up to the house I would see new life, new growth—tall grasses and flowers blowing in the breeze. But I also wanted to create a memorial garden whose centerpiece would be a "memory bench" dedicated to Bernie to help keep his memory alive.

I bought a plain concrete, curved bench that would sit nicely under a tree, and placed it in the new landscaping. When I would come home or go out my front door I was so happy to see the garden and the bench. But my contentment was short-lived—Bernie's bench was not "alive" enough. Then at a family retreat with my youngest daughter, I found my inspiration for how to make it come to life. As we'd walked the campgrounds, we'd seen a mosaic wall that had been added to yearly by a new visiting group. That was it—we would mosaic the bench.

On the Thanksgiving weekend at my house, my children and my close cousins and I (with the help of a talented friend) created a beautiful, highly personal, mosaic bench. For two hours, 16 loving hands set memorabilia—Bernie's YMCA card, a guitar pick, my Girl Scout pin, a

Dodger pin, a UCLA pin—and tiles, including pieces of a souvenir vase that belonged to my parents and a ceramic cup that one of my daughters made in preschool, into the top of the bench. But the concept of "Bernie's bench" had changed. It had evolved to become something that honors not just my husband, but also my parents, my children, my grandchild and me, even my grandson's dog—the whole family.

Now when I look at the beautiful bench, which I moved to the front porch, I can almost feel the memories come to life—the dog barking, the guitar pick picking, Bernie enjoying an afternoon at Dodger Stadium.... I can feel everyone.

"Rather than mourn the loss of a flame, remember, and celebrate how brightly it burned."

—Buddie Shrier

Life Lesson

I want to cherish and live happily with my memories. But I don't ever want to be stuck in the past. The past will always be with me, but I am looking forward to creating new memories. I think that is a good way to go through the healing process: allowing past memories to be the foundation on which to create new ones.

11. Hey, You in the Mirror, You're Doing Okay!

Having Compassion for Myself

I HAVE LEFT the front door open and even left the keys in the door. I cannot balance my checking account, and I really have been trying. I've overfilled the pool. I've left the skylight open during the rain. Once I left the bathroom heater on for four days.

I could have agonized about any of those things (especially the electricity bill for leaving the bathroom heater on), but then I would have been upset, and I don't like to be upset. I could have spent hours trying to figure out where I messed up with the bank balance, but I'd just be frustrated. I don't want to frustrate myself. Instead, I let it go.

Well, not exactly. I gave my checking account to the bank to figure out. I opened a second checking account and started fresh. When the bank lost interest in my discrepancy, a dear friend who likes numbers said she would balance it. Four weeks later, she and her husband arrived with my bankbook and reams of paper in hand and said, "You forgot to add Bernie's Social Security deposit." Problem solved!

I think we need to have compassion for ourselves and where we're at. It doesn't matter if we're grieving or not. But it seems that having compassion for one's self is one of the hardest things to do. Most of us seem to prefer being hard on ourselves—looking in the mirror and saying, "My hair doesn't look good…this is wrong…that is wrong.…" We don't say, "Hello mirror, you look really good!" Instead, it's "Why are you doing this? Why don't you lose weight? Why aren't you more disciplined?" We rarely say it's okay for us to be where we are in any moment.

At the pace most of us go, we don't always stop to consider what we have accomplished. I often think that if I were to put two lists on a sheet of paper under the headings What I Did Today and What I Didn't Do Today, the "dids" would probably outnumber the "didn'ts."

You know the saying, "Don't take yourself or life too seriously"? There is truth in this. If you are hard on yourself and don't laugh at the stupid things you do or at your failures, it can only eat away at you. (I like eating—I just don't want anything or anyone to eat me!) As my mother used to say, "It's never as good as it seems, and it's never as bad as it seems."

"Don't take yourself or life too seriously."
—Buddie Shrier

A Story on My Journey…

The Kvetching Bear

I missed not having someone to complain to. Every morning when I woke up with Bernie I told him what part of my body hurt—my shoulder, I slept wrong, my foot, I don't know…. I really think I enjoy complaining. (I have a girlfriend whose husband says that if she wakes up without a complaint, he'll know she's dead.) Now I didn't have anyone to listen to me. So I asked myself how I could I solve this.

Well, I wasn't going to journal my complaints—that sounded really awful! I couldn't just telephone a friend for a morning complaint. So I decided to go in search of an "autograph animal" like the kind I'd had as a kid—a stuffed animal I'd take to school so my friends could write on it.

I got a bear, twelve inches tall, and he's kind of soft and wonderful and has a little brown nose and you can write on him, and he's holding three balloons—yellow, blue and red—and it says "Congratulations" on his tummy. I thought, what a nice way to wake up in the morning—"Congratulations, you got through another day!" I keep my bear on my bed, and when I wake up, if I want to complain, he's holding his little pen, and I write, "My shoulder [or whatever] hurts."

Actually I got two bears. My kids said I needed five, but I've started off with two. If I were an inventor, I'd invent a grieving bear, or a complaining bear, and call him Oy Vey. Everyone can use a bear, right?

Life Lesson

My goal is to be in the present and have compassion for myself in the moment. I've learned not to be so hard on myself—I can't always have it together. This realization is necessary to get from Point A to Point B. I also know it's good to stop at the end of the day or the end of the week and ask, "What have I learned?" I might do it once a day or once a week when I sit quietly during meditation or prayer. Then I can be thankful for what I have accomplished.

12. I Didn't Ask to Become an Expert on Grieving

Trusting the Process

SOME DAYS I'd say, "I don't want this!" Or I'd ask, "Why me? Why am I not going to be able to go through life holding hands with my mate?" But the choice wasn't given to me. There are no answers for those questions. I need to believe that for some reason I was given this, that this is a path that is going to bring me wisdom and understanding.

When Bernie died, I was unable to experience the small, ordinary happenings of life because of the piercing pain of loss I felt. But somehow, through the pain, I began to hear my mother's words— "Let go and let God." One bit at a time, one day at a time, as I let go of my pain and remembered to have compassion for myself, I started to hear and understand what my mother meant. Her words of wisdom became a part of my very essence.

And I thought of my father. My father had just lost his leg when we learned that my mother had brain and lung cancer. Two months later, when my mother died, Dad, who was confined to a wheelchair, sat there for a short while then said, "What's going to happen to me?" But I took his words as a message that he wanted to live, that he was going to survive, because he wasn't just grieving for his wife—he was thinking of himself. My father came to live with Bernie and me for five years, happily wheeling himself around and greeting every day with "Look how beautiful it is!" One day he said to me, "What happens if I lose the other leg?" and answered himself: "It's going to be really difficult." I was thinking, "You won't have either leg, and you're still willing to live?" He was willing to live to the very end. That was a lesson that I will never forget.

Six months after my husband died was the first time I went to his gravesite. I felt it was going to be very, very difficult, and that no one should go with me. My main reason for going then was that I was so afraid of going.

The anticipation was worse than being there. When I was standing at the gravesite, I was less afraid and less emotional than I thought I would be. The location was so beautiful. When I sat down, I could see where the casket had made lines in the grass, and I could see the grass growing over. I knew the next time I came the lines would be fainter. I thought about some words of wisdom that a good friend gave me. She'd found them copied out by her mother after her mother had died.

Do not stand at my grave and weep. I am not there. I do not sleep. I am a thousand winds that blow. I am the diamond glint on snow. I am the sunlight on ripened grain. I am the gentle autumn rain. When you awaken in the morning light, I am light. I am the swift uplifting rush of quiet birds in circled flight. I am the song of soft life of the star that shines at night. Do not stand at my grave and cry. I am not there. I did not die.
—author unknown

People say it gets better with time, and I've come to believe it does. I think the most important part of the grieving process is learning to trust, opening up to trust. Then, piece by piece, it's possible to begin to re-enter the world.

"Let go and let God."
—Buddie Shrier

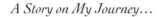

A Story on My Journey…

The Rain

It started on a Wednesday. Thursday, Friday and Saturday it rained and rained and rained some more. There was no sun whatsoever. It reminded me of what my grief felt like when Bernie died. It was so heavy and wouldn't stop. You couldn't even breathe—the air was that heavy. People were worried about mudslides, trees falling. I just wanted to be held or huddle in my home and try to protect myself.

Then the heavy rain changed. It became the most interesting rain I had ever experienced. It was light rain, and then a few minutes later the sun would shine, and then it would rain again. In my front yard it was raining and in my back yard the sun was out. You didn't know what it was going to do. But it was okay, because I knew it would stop and the sun would come out. The heaviness, where I couldn't breathe and I couldn't get out from underneath it, was no longer there. That rain–sun–rain–sun reminded me of one thing: growth. Of plants and blossoming and the cycle of life. In order for the earth to accept all the rain, you have to give it a chance to breathe. And once it accepts it, a flower can start to blossom because it's getting what it needs—the sun and the rain. If it gets just the rain, a plant will die. It will get so soaked its roots will rot.

I felt that the weather was telling me I must acknowledge the grief and then let it go. Let go of that rain and
that heaviness, and allow the sunshine to come in. Then I
could start to blossom.

*"Our guardian angels have eyes that see,
ears that hear, hearts that feel and hands
that touch."*

—Buddie Shrier

Life Lesson

When will the mourning end? I think people in mourning have to come to grips with death before they can live again. Mourning doesn't end after a year; that's a fantasy. It can go on for years and years. I think you need to mourn at your own pace. Mourning ends when people realize that they can live again, that they can concentrate their energies on their lives, and not just on their pain.

I do believe in the process; I believe in the healing. I believe that if you trust the process of time healing, if you trust that the sun will shine again, the process works.

Living in Light...

---

*"The light of the sun is but the shadow of love....
Love is the wind, the tide, the waves, the
sunshine. Its power is incalculable."*

—Henry David Thoreau
Paradise (To Be) Regained

13. One Year Later

I Am Not the Same Sissy

JUNE 3, 2006, was the unveiling of Bernie's headstone, almost exactly a year after he died. Anticipation is scarier than facing anything. I knew I'd cry. But I put one foot in front of the other and I managed.

I looked at my three daughters—one who had been married for six years, one soon to be married, and another not yet married—and realized I am the one they looked to for guidance. I needed to continue to be a good example to them. I wanted to show them how you go through life, or the next day, or the next hour, making yourself as whole and complete as possible under adversity.

If I really had any advice at that moment for them, or for anyone, it was that when you're so aware of what you've lost, turn that around and ask what you have gained. And so the unveiling became not just a day of thinking about our loss. It became one of contemplation about what had been gained.

I couldn't believe it had been a year. Bernie's death still feels like a dream; it's surreal. There have been moments, like watching a beautiful sunset, when I would think he's going to be there and see it with me. Or when that first rose blooms in the garden. I would have gone into the house and said, "You have got to come out here and see this. It's so perfect, so beautiful." Or when I see that starry sky, because we used to sit in the Jacuzzi and look up at the sky and really talk.

I know he's not here, but I still hope to wake up in the morning and the bed is going to be unmade on his side, and it's all just going to be a bad dream. The thing that I do know is that he is not coming back. I think if the first year teaches anything, it's the finality of it: that I would still have all those hopes and dreams I'd had, but I would have them without my partner.

I looked at the year and I thought to myself, "You know, I'm okay. I can do this." I was more comfortable than I thought I'd be. I felt proud of myself for the things that I could do—I could sleep at night, pay the taxes, and the house hadn't fallen on my head. My family needs me and my community needs me. And I need them. I'm not saying that I can do it all alone, but I can certainly pick up the phone and ask someone to help me. I can do it as long as I have people to call upon for help.

I think about the little things that I thought were important a year ago that now are not. You balance your checkbook or you don't balance your checkbook. You take out the trash or you don't. You can leave your house a mess. You don't have to be so hard on yourself. This realization is important.

And I've realized that just as there are a lot of books on mourning, there are a lot of ways you can approach moving forward. You learn new ways of coping. We don't usually acknowledge our own growth. It's like the miracle of a child's first step. It's a big deal the first time, but then we don't see the miracle of the child continuing to walk.

There are still lots of things that I am scared to do. I don't see plays alone; it hurts to think that I've got to find someone to go with. It's like making dinner reservations for five, not for six. It just hits so hard. I travel, but without a camera. I'm afraid to see he's not there.

At the one-year point I haven't taken off my wedding ring. In the bereavement group, they said you'll

know when you're ready to take it off. I guess for me it'll be when I'm mentally and emotionally ready. Right now the community is so strong in my life, and people—men, women—just mean so much to me, and I have companionship with couples, so I don't feel I lack having a particular man in my life. I think I have to go on this journey alone before I can open up to someone else. I have to get to the bottom, feel all the feelings, hurt with all the hurt, ride the wave of knowing I'm not part of a couple, and then climb up before I can be emotionally available for another relationship.

It's interesting. I miss him a lot. I have a real void because he's not here. But I don't feel sorry for myself. I don't know if this is strange or not. Perhaps it's because I have accepted the opportunity to develop a new me. I feel cheated in that I wanted more time, but I don't feel sorry for myself. We had such a rich marriage, and I continue to have a rich life. I feel lucky that nothing was unresolved in our life together. Maybe that's why I feel I can write this book—because we said everything that needed to be said, we did everything that we needed to do.

That doesn't mean I don't cry. I still cry a lot, but it's become less deep, not to the core. I know that God wants a human being to live in light, to be illuminated. I know that eventually I can live in light, because I see people whom this has happened to who live in light.

So, yeah, the worst has happened! Nothing else can happen that is worse than this. And I've lived through it, which means I can live through anything. I am a powerful human being. I choose to live, not to die.

Everyone says that the second year is going to get a bit easier. But I think it's a bit scary. What's tomorrow going to bring? One thing that is not going to be different is that the sun is going to shine again. And so will I.

A Story on My Journey…

Cycle of Love

My youngest daughter, Nadine, and her fiancé, Zach, were able to ask for Bernie's blessing of their marriage shortly before he died. He happily gave it, and the union was blessed, with Zach giving Nadine an engagement ring crafted out of my engagement ring and his grandmother's gold wedding band. (The happy couple told Bernie that because he had such a successful marriage, they wanted his advice. Bernie thought for a moment. His advice to them was: Never go to bed angry, don't take yourself or life too seriously, and have patience with your pain-in-the-ass mother-in-law. He had a sense of humor till the end.)

Nadine and Zach's wedding took place a little more than a year after Bernie died, three weeks after Bernie's unveiling. It was a delicate balancing act because I wanted to acknowledge that my children were still grieving just as deeply as I was. I wanted the wedding to be a celebration, yet still honor Bernie. So we planned for it to be as much a family affair as possible. We wanted Bernie present in spirit, and we didn't want to emphasize his absence. There was no procession—my four-year-old-grandson walked Nadine down the aisle. (I didn't want to because it would have been too painful.) There was no first dance and no speeches. During the ceremony, the entire family was under the *chuppah* (wedding arch). Bernie's *talis* (prayer shawl) was wrapped around them. After, we celebrated in the back yard of my eldest daughter's house.

My greatest fear about the wedding had been that people would be sad for our family. That didn't happen. We partied as a complete family, dancing and laughing long into the night. And I knew, we are still a whole family.

Life Lesson

It would be easy to shut down. It would be easy to pull the covers over my head. I could ignore the learning and hang on to my original vision of myself and my world and the way I thought it would be. But that's not the path that yields wisdom and understanding. It's a choice. If you choose life—and I'm choosing to be alive—then you choose to grow and develop and move on. My goals are goals of growth. I'm proud of myself. I'm becoming the person I was destined to be.

Celebrating Bernie Taran

Bernie Taran, 1939–2005

My Husband,
a Wonderful, Loving, Generous, Simple Man

WHEN BERNIE became sick, we wallpapered his home office from floor to ceiling with "get well" cards. During his month-long stay in the hospital, I stuck up hundreds and hundreds of them. I'd expected cards from family and close friends, but—from the pharmacy? The fire department? Why did so many people care about my simple husband? The answer is in the message of one of those cards: "Bernie is a doer, a giver and a *mensch*." He cared deeply for his family, his friends, his community, and was always doing something for others.

A generous and tireless volunteer, he was the go-to person for getting things done. He always stepped up to the plate and said "yes." That is how he became the president of MERRAG (the local emergency response group), and why he drove for the Braille Institute. He was a mentor to a young boy and a reading tutor to elementary school children. He was on the board of the Anti-Defamation League, was a past president of B'nai B'rith Lodge, organizer of the charitable B'nai B'rith Texas Hold

'Em Poker Tournament, and on the national board of Hadassah's Associates.

What was remarkable about Bernie's giving was that he never asked for or needed any type of recognition. He loved being behind the scenes and making things happen. He did it because he loved people, and he loved helping.

At six feet four inches, my husband stood out. However, it was not merely for his height, but his demeanor. The man we affectionately called Berndog was big, strong and full of life, though he was a gentle giant. He always wore a smile on his face and would talk to anyone who paused to listen. To say that Bernie loved to talk is putting it mildly. He was a master storyteller. Mention any subject—from stocks to "Sex in the City"—and he could begin a story that would go on and on, asking questions and answering them himself. But with us at home he would often sit quietly, just sharing the space.

He loved the simple pleasures of life—a good hamburger (especially one from Fatburger), deli food, free samples at Costco, poker, hiking in the hills of Santa Barbara, walking in the neighborhood in a dusty T-shirt and shorts listening on headphones to books on tape.

There was nothing complicated about Bernie—about Bernie the human being, Bernie the father, Bernie the husband. He just didn't carry any baggage. When we married, he was 38 (it was his first marriage, my second), and I became the center of his universe. He loved me with a love that was simple, a love that was unconditional. He wasn't conventionally romantic, but he expressed his love in everything he did for me. He showed it when he put gas in my car, when he arrived at six in the morning to help me set up for an event, and when he would karaoke and dance with me even though he was tone deaf and had no rhythm. Our life was about being together. "Bernie and Sissy," "Sissy and Bernie"—it was almost like one word. In Bernie I was lucky enough to find my soul mate.

When he retired at 50, it was because he wanted to be with me and our three daughters. (Also because he wanted to wear shorts and T-shirts and sleep in late.) He never missed the events in the girls' lives—the ball games, the soccer matches, the PTA meetings, the field trips. He helped work the concession stand at the high school volleyball and football games; he was the PTA treasurer. That was how he wanted to live.

Rabbi Steve remarked that Bernie would never have considered himself a philosopher, but that his life was "a series of profoundly wise and moral decisions." Somehow Bernie always knew the right decisions to make. Where other men might retire at the age of 65 and have 15 years of retirement, he retired at 50 and got his 15 years in. He

got his time with his children. He and I traveled everywhere we wanted, we laughed a lot, we said everything we wanted. It wasn't that he didn't want more, or that I didn't. Of course he wanted more. But I believe that he didn't have any issues to resolve because somehow, intuitively, he seemed to have planned out his life. He lived his life exactly as he wanted to.

Bernie didn't know he was going to die, even right at the end. He'd never thought about death, and he really didn't have a fear of it. He didn't need to make peace with people, or ask for forgiveness to be able to let go. And none of us felt that we had to hold on to him. He'd lived a great life. He could go in peace. My gift to him is to live.

Happiness

by Bernie Taran

What makes me happy? I feel different kinds of happiness. When my team scores a touchdown, or wins a game, or I win a bet, or see a good movie, or have a nice dinner, or hundreds of other everyday events occur, it makes me happy. I call these "momentary" or "short-term" happiness. And they make life enjoyable.

Getting a pay raise, seeing my children's bat mitzvahs, winning an award or having my children or wife win an award, milestone events (graduations, passing the bar, acceptance to colleges, etc.), a great vacation, and many other events make me happy. I call these "feel good all over" happiness. Not only do these make life more enjoyable, but they stay with me for a long time. Whenever I think of these events I feel happy.

The best happiness is that which comes with being content with myself and enjoying and appreciating everyday living. I have this happiness because I've been lucky in finding a wonderful wife who makes my life happy. And because of her we have wonderful children who bring us joy. I call this true happiness.

—Bernie Taran, 2000

Papa Berndog

As I walked Mount Sinai Cemetery, I saw on grave mark-
ers words such as "beloved son, father, grandfather," and
I was a little bothered by that. I wanted Bernie's marker
to be more personable and also not as serious. I know
that sounds strange, but in our relationship we laughed
and played around a lot, so I wanted something he would
approve of. We wrote:

Bernard L. Taran

February 9, 1939–June 1, 2005

A gentle giant. A hug and a smile for everyone.

We will miss you, Papa Berndog.

Even when I say it, it brings a smile instead of a tear
to me.

Appendix A

Books That Helped Me Heal,
an Annotated List

THE FOLLOWING books especially helped me during my first year of grieving:

Singer, Lilly; Sirot, Margaret; Rodd, Susan. *Beyond Loss: A Practical Guide Through Grief to a Meaningful Life.* Santa Barbara, California: Blue Point Books, 2002. This became my resource during the early weeks. It is organized in a concise way that I could relate to and showed me what needed to be done and when. It helped me to begin focusing on each day.

Hickman, Martha Whitmore. *Healing after Loss.* New York: Perennial, 1994. This book is more than meditations. Each page has a quote from somebody, famous or not, then Hickman's interpretation of it, and then there is a daily practice for the reader. I found myself reading it every night before I went to bed. The readings got me thinking about my day, and made each day end on a powerful note of contemplation about where I was, where I'd been, where I was going.

Brener, Anne. *Mourning and Mitzvah: A Guided Journal for Walking the Mourner's Path Through Grief to Healing.* Woodstock, Vermont: Jewish Lights Publishing, 1993. I found this book extremely user-friendly, in an easy-to-read format. It is a journal of guided exercises that does not have to be read page by page. I skipped around and did readings and exercises as I needed and often revisited sections when an issue surfaced.

Wolfson, Dr. Ron. *A Time to Mourn, a Time to Comfort.* Woodstock, Vermont: Jewish Lights Publishing, 1993. I used this as a resource for any questions I had about the Jewish approach to death and dying. It helped explain Jewish rituals and the healing process.

Rando, Therese A., Ph.D. *How to Go on Living When Someone You Love Dies.* New York: Bantam Books, 1991. More scientific than the others, this book has a clinical approach to death and dying. It shows different forms of grief and explains them thoroughly. It includes a comprehensive resource list of help and support groups.

Colgrove, Melba, Ph.D.; Bloomfield, Harold H., M.D.; McWilliams, Peter. *How to Survive the Loss of a Love.* New York: Bantam Books, 1977. The subtitle of this short, simple book is *58 Things to Do When There Is Nothing to Be Done*. It gives lists, short poems and easy suggestions. (It even congratulated me when I finished reading its 117 pages!)

Bozarth, Alla Renée, Ph.D. *A Journey Through Grief.* Center City, Minnesota: Hazelden, 1990. Dr. Bozarth, a therapist and Episcopal priest, writes about her own experiences and journeys using poetry and short stories.

Appendix B

My Mother's Legacy

MY MOTHER, Buddie Shrier, was a woman who loved life and people and making the world a better place. She never sat on the sidelines. She always seemed to have the right thing to say, to everyone. I'd like to honor my mother's memory here by sharing with you a little of her most important advice.

The following was written by my mother in reference to *her* mother, my grandmother Lillian Schwartz.

The Gospel of the One-Step

When I was growing up, who was a girl's number one teacher? Her Jewish mother, of course. One of my favorite lessons was a dance Mother called the One-Step, which, through the years, has glided me over many a bumpy floor. I've come 'round to calling it the Gospel of the One-Step because what my mother said was "gospel." I'd love to teach you how to do it, and here's how:

  1. Resolve to see your work, your task—no matter how big—in terms of one day's work, one duty, at a time.

2. Resolve to handle any trouble or sorrow or temptation for this one day. Don't continue to carry yesterday's burden; don't try to imagine what tomorrow holds.

3. Resolve to take one step now *toward being a better person. If you know one thing you could do now—then do it! And then you'll know what the next step should be, and you'll have the power to take it.*

That's what my mother said!

Twelve years ago, after my mother died, I photocopied and framed my grandmother's "Gospel" (written out in my mother's handwriting) and gave one to each of my daughters.

My Mother's Path to Self-Esteem

My mother always knew how to help make someone feel good about herself or himself. If she felt someone's self-confidence needed a boost, she would pass along this list.

Twenty-One Ways to Increase Self-Esteem

1. Smile at yourself in the mirror.

2. Close your eyes and feel the warmth in your heart.

3. Imagine inside you a little child whom you love.

4. Accept a compliment with deservedness.

5. Smile at someone you don't know.

6. Imagine people liking you as they pass you on the street.

7. Tell the truth.

8. Express yourself.

9. Feel your feelings and acknowledge them.

10. State your opinion without making anyone wrong.

11. Have fun.

12. Spend an appropriate amount of money on yourself.

13. Tell someone what you like about them.

14. Tell yourself what you like about yourself.

15. Make a list of things you like about yourself.

16. Read it out loud.

17. Say it in front of a mirror.

18. Stand before a mirror until you are not judging yourself.

19. See yourself perfect as you are.

20. Notice how lovable you are.

21. Recognize your exquisite uniqueness.

"Look in the mirror without looking for what's wrong."

—Buddie Shrier

After my mother died, I found the following in her box of writings. And if you read to the end, you'll see where the title of this book came from.

My Wish List for You

by Buddie Shrier

I want you to be happy. I want you to fill your heart with feelings of wonder and to be full of courage and hope. I want you to have the type of friendship that is a treasure, and the kind of love that is beautiful forever. I wish you contentment—the sweet, quiet, inner kind that comes around and never goes away.

I want you to have hopes and have them all come true. I want you to make the most of this moment in time. I want you to have a real understanding of how unique and rare you truly are. I want to remind you that the sun may disappear for a while, but it never forgets to shine. I want you to have faith. May you have feelings that are shared from heart to heart—simple pleasures amidst this complex world, and wonderful goals that are within your grasp. May the words you listen to say the things you need to hear. And may a cheerful face lovingly look back at you when you happen to glance in your mirror.

I wish you the insight to see your inner and outer beauty. I wish you sweet dreams. I want you to have times when you feel

like singing and dancing and laughing out loud. I want you to be able to make your good times better, and your hard times easier to handle. I want you to have millions of moments when you find satisfaction in the things you do so wonderfully. And I wish I could find a way to tell you—in untold ways—how important you are to me.

Of all the things I'll be wishing for, wherever you are and whatever I may do, there will never be a day in my life when I won't be wishing for the best—for you.

P.S. Tomorrow the sun will shine, and so will you.